YOUNG ADVENTURER'S ALPHABET

AF261315

Written & Illustrated

by

Benjamin Wallace

© 2013 Benjamin Wallace.
All rights reserved.

All images copyrighted by Benjamin Wallace.

This book or any portion thereof may not be reproduced or used in any manner whatsoever
without the express written permission of the publisher.

Printed in the United States of America

First Printing, 2013

ISBN-13: 978-1492809791
ISBN-10: 1492809799

www.BenjaminWallaceBooks.com

To my kids,
I finally wrote a book that you're allowed to read.
I love you all.

Amazon

A is for Amazon, a river so grand
there's only one bigger in all of the land.
It crashes down mountains and cuts through the hills.
It passes through jungles, and flows further still,
through towns and past beaches and into the sea.
And it keeps flowing still; it's so big, you see?

It's in South America, below the equator.
And, you should go see it sooner or later.
It's hot and it's muggy, but well worth the trip.
You can't take a car there. There isn't a bridge.

The river's so wide, a mile at the least,
that there's no way to cross it using only your feet.
You'll need a boat, a barge, or canoe.
You could try to swim it, but let me warn you:

There're fish in the river—fish that are bite-y,
They call them piranha and you can't take them lightly.
They've got teeth like sharks and they swim up in droves.
And, they'll make you their meal if you swim in the coves.

But, if you stay on the shore you're really quite safe.
Except from the jaguars, cougars, and snakes,
and poisonous tree frogs, and vampire bats,
and, though monkeys won't bite, they might take your hat.

So, keep your eyes open when you visit this river,
and walk extra careful so you don't become dinner.

Boomerang

B is for boomerang, the stick that returns.
You throw it away and it twists and it turns
in a circular motion it wobbles around
and comes back to your hand or lands on the ground.

They're used in Australia, the down under place,
with kangaroos, wallabies and plenty of space.
They call it the outback, a desert so vast,
that there's no way across or around it that's fast.

Stroll for a walk-a-bout or dive in the sea.
There's plenty to do and lots to go see.
But, watch out for snakes; they'll probably bite.
And, if you go snorkeling, beware the Great White.

Don't leave without grabbing a great souvenir
to remember the fun and prove you were here.
If you pick up a boomerang and hurl it a bit,
and it doesn't come back, you just bought a stick.

Cannibal

C is for Cannibal, a right hungry bunch.
And if you should meet them they'll have you for lunch.
We're not talking sandwiches, salads and such.
We're talking you, breaded and stuffed.

They've got a big pot called the kid cooker pro.
They'll nab you and lash you and in it you'll go.
They'll light a big fire to warm up the water,
and you'll start to roast as it starts to get hotter.

And there you will simmer, until they eat dinner,
stewing in carrots and roots.
So, if you don't escape you'll be put on a plate
and end up as somebody's toots.

So, don't trust a cannibal if he smiles when he meets you.
Though he seems friendly, he just wants to eat you.

Dynamite

D is for Dynamite, the stick that explodes.
It looks like a candle, but everyone knows
when you light it, it sparkles and hisses in fits
then it burns down and blows itself up to bits.

It's used to build roads, move mountains and more.
And dig in the Earth to find gold, gems and ore.
They bury and blast it and everything flies
and great rolls of thunder fill up the skies.

Before they explode it, they yell, "Fire in the hole!"
They then drop the plunger, so do what you're told.
Because stuff will go flying when they light that stick.
So get behind cover and plug your ears quick.

If you ever see some get away soon.
Because KABOOM and KABLAMMO, KA-DANG, BANG and BOOM
and BOOSH, CRASH and BAM, WHAM, GADOOSH and SHADOOM!

TNT
TNT
TNT
TNT
TNT
FLASHLIGHT
CANDLES

Everest

E is for Everest, the world's tallest mountain.
If you're counting in feet, you'll count to the thousands.
It's twenty-nine thousand and twenty-nine feet
from the base of the ground to the top of the peak.

And climbing's the only way to get there.
But if you go to the top you'll need your own air.
The air is so thin, so high up there, you see.
There's not enough oxygen in it to breathe.

If you're planning on climbing into the sky
hire a Sherpa and he'll be your guide.
He'll show you the way to get to the top
and help you stay safe so you never drop.

Watch out for the Yeti, that mythical beast.
He lives in the high Himalayan peaks.
We don't really know if he's real or fake.
But is it a chance that you're willing to take?

Freighter

F is for Freighter, because you might need a ship
to bring back the stuff that you found on your trip.

An idol's too big to fit on a plane.
And, if there's an ocean to cross, you can't take a train.

A car just won't do to carry your treasure.
And you can't really just walk back from wherever.

A ship is just perfect, though it is kind of slow.
So bring something to read or do as you go.

You could use the time to plan your next trip,
because there's not much to do when you're on a ship.

VEN
JIG
ROMA

Gorilla

G is for Gorilla, the largest of apes
and it's more than their size that makes them so great.
They're also quite smart. So smart, in fact,
that they can use tools and most apes can't do that.

They live high in the mountains.
They live low in the swamps.
They live in forests and jungles.
They live wherever they want.

They can weigh more than 400 pounds
and it's mostly all muscle they carry around.
They eat lots of fruits and they eat some ants
but, it's hard to get fat if you mostly eat plants.

They live in a troop and wander around
looking for food they can find on the ground.
And if they find trouble, like a leopard or croc,
they bring out the big guy to pound it a lot.

He's easy to spot because he'll have big teeth
and a white patch of fur down his back to his feet.
It's the Silverback's job to keep the troop safe.
He is the first to rise up and get in your face.

So walk on by softly, don't point and don't stare.
But if he should see you—GET OUT OF THERE!

Howdah

H is for Howdah, and would you look at that?
It's a carriage that sits on an elephant's back.
I can't even imagine who travels up there
so high off the ground for the whole world to stare.

But it seems like a strange way to travel around.
And what would you do when you want to get down?
Does the elephant know when you've finally arrived?
And use it's great trunk to get you outside?

It's not like a saddle, not some simple seat.
The way this thing looks, it's hard to be beat.
It's covered with carvings and painted like gold.
And not everyone has one. That's what I'm told.

Maybe a prince or a king or a queen
would ride up in there when they want to be seen.
They'd travel the streets on an elephant's back
and wave to the crowd. Or would they even do that?

They'd probably just sit there and take in the view.
And make the elephant trumpet to make people move.
And look down on the crowd at the elephant's feet.
As it left giant messes behind in the street.

As neat as it is, it seems kind of mean
to ride on an elephant just to be seen.
And it's a ridiculous way to get to the market.
When you ride on an elephant, where do you park it?

Iditarod

I is for Iditarod, a race through wind and snow.
If you're going to run it, there are a few things you should know.

It happens in Alaska, the biggest state around.
And, the whole time that you're racing, there's snow upon the ground.

The race begins in Anchorage and ends in a place called Nome.
And both of these cities are a long, long way from home.

You won't need your sneakers or fancy running shoes.
But some nice warm boots will keep all your toes from turning blue.

You ride upon a sled, you see, for the distance of the race.
And a team of dogs will pull you as the snow blows in your face.

16 dogs make up the team and pull you day and night.
Hook up your team, holler "mush!" and hang on really tight.

It takes a week of days, or more, just to win the race.
Sometimes it takes twenty-three to finish in last place.

It's forty nine and a thousand miles to reach the finish line.
And you'll be cold and wet almost the entire time.

So grab your hat, and scarf, and gloves, and some extra socks.
But don't forget, even if you win, this race is for the dogs.

Jump

J is for Jump,
because you might have to leap
off a bridge or a ledge or over a creek
or into a river, a lake or a sea
or into a hut, or a boat or a tree
or over a wall, a log or ravine
or into a cave, or a truck or a stream
or under a rock or from the end of a dock
or off of a trestle that's starting to rock
or up to the top of a really tall spot
to hide from a hippo, a rhino or croc
or a snake, or a lion, or a giant stampede
of elephants, elks or scared wildebeests
because, sometimes, just running isn't enough
and in times like those you'll just have to jump.

K is for Kayak, a boat built for one.
And they're just perfect, if you've got a river to run.

They're small and they're nimble.
They're light and they're quick.
But, you've got to be careful,
They're easy to tip.

They're great for the rivers you might have to float.
And they can go places too small for a boat.

They're perfect for rapids,
rocks, drops and all.
But always get out
before hitting the falls.

Lava

L is for Lava, and this stuff is hot.
So hot, in fact, that it's just melted rock.
It glows in the dark, it's so full of heat.
Its temperature reaches two thousand degrees.

It's found in volcanoes, and if you find it—GO!
Because when a volcano erupts the lava will flow.
It flows in rivers and gathers in lakes
and pools inside mountains until there are quakes.

The ground will tremble. The mountain will roar.
And then blow its top causing lava to pour.
It will spout in the air for hundreds of feet
and rain down the volcano under your feet.

It will run down the side, melting rocks, burning trees.
And often won't stop until it reaches the sea.
And there it will cool and turn into the shore.
And it will stop being lava and become rock once more.

Monsoon

M is for Monsoon, and you're going to get drenched.
Because once this thing starts, it goes on without end.
The rain falls forever, or so it would seem
since enough of it falls to turn deserts green.

It happens in Asia and Africa, too.
Every year, just like clockwork, you'll get a monsoon.
The rains will fall down and the plants will sprout up.
It goes on for a season. Just raining and stuff.

The rains bring relief and water for crops.
But sometimes it feels like it just never stops.
Falling and falling for days without end
with nothing to do but watch it come in.

Then, all of a sudden, it just kind of stops.
People go out and they harvest the crops.
And the weather turns warmer and incredibly dry
and you find yourself hoping for some rain from the sky.

Nomad

N is for Nomad, these folks get around.
They don't live in a house, a city or town.
They wander the desert, the plains and the steppes
looking for food and living in tents.

The places they live get dry really quick.
And so, every year, they go on a trip.
They go with their families, their neighbors and friends
and follow the rains until the dry season ends.

They travel by camel, or horse, or canoe.
Sometimes they just walk. That's just what they do.
And they take everything with them. Their tents are their home.
They even bring herds of cattle and goats.

They travel in tribes of family and friends.
And travel thousands of miles before it all ends.
They then turn around and head back where they began.
Until they pack up and start over again.

Outrigger

O is for Outrigger, an odd little ship.
It just kind of looks like a boat and a bit.
It's one part canoe. That part we've seen.
But what's with the thing at the end of the beam?

It's too small to sit in and couldn't hold much.
It's there on the side to hold the boat up.
It gives the boat balance and keeps you up straight
because this boat's built for oceans, not rivers or lakes.

They've been used forever to cross thousands of miles
across Polynesia and other famed isles.
They're sturdy in waves and less likely to tip
which would be a disaster for you on your trip.

And, if you need to run, it might do the trick.
These little boats are incredibly quick.
Because they're so narrow in both of their parts
they slip through the water like a couple of darts.

So if you ever look back and find that you're being chased
just keep on paddling until you escape.

Pyramid

P is for Pyramid, those big pointy things
that they built in the deserts to bury their kings.
They're made out of stone that was cut down by hand
and stacked up together on top of the sand.

The biggest of all is in Egypt today.
And because of its size, it's likely to stay.
It reaches a height of almost 500 feet
and for quite some time that couldn't be beat.

For three thousand eight hundred and probably more years
it rose from the Earth without any peers.
The tallest thing made, ever, by man
to bury a king—just one—in the sand.

They then filled it up with mummies and coffers
and spread rumors of curses to discourage grave robbers.
They loaded the inside with pots, jewels and gold
and sealed it all up for all to behold.

The tomb could be seen from miles away.
It was just as big then as it is today.
But when it was first built, it was covered in white
and polished so fine that it lit up at night.

Over the years, time took its toll.
That's why it ended up looking so old.
People kept looking for mummies and treasure
and ruined a bit of our history forever.

You can go see it. It's still there today.
It will be eons before it goes away.
But if you should visit the ancient world's wonder
don't climb to the top. The good stuff's found under.

Quicksand

Q is for Quicksand, and boy is it quick.
Before you know it you're up to your hips.
And if you struggle and squirm, each little bit
will pull you down further, till your up to your lips.

Try and stay calm and float to the land.
Quicksand is just water filled up with sand.
Then grab on to a vine, but, make no mistake,
things will get worse if it's really a snake.

Research

R is for Research. Your quest begins here.
In a library filled with books through the years.
They're musty and dusty. They're heavy and thick.
But they could be the start of your adventurous trip.

Treasures are buried in stories and myths,
tall tales told to children, in parts and in bits.
The clue could be there in a poem or a song
or a map or a chart tucked away for too long.

Adventure is hidden in history's shadows.
A hint could be found in the recounting of battles.
Or a legend long lost, once thought to be lies
could hold the key to your next great prize.

So pore into the books and tear through the pages.
There could be a treasure that's been hidden for ages.
But remember this please, don't shout when you find it.
You're still in a library. You've got to be quiet.

Shipwrecked

S is for Shipwrecked and it's as bad as it sounds.
It happens to folks when their boats run aground.
If it happens to you when you're out at sea
you'd better get swimming and head for a beach.

If it's an island, you might wait a bit
for someone to find you or send out a ship.
So, it's time to start making yourself right at home
and thinking up games you can play all alone.

You're going to need shelter, a roof and a bed.
Water and food for the long days ahead.
There'll probably be coconuts lying around
so gather whatever you find on the ground.

You'll need a fire to stay warm at night.
So pile the wood and look for a light.
If you have a match that could do the trick.
But you'll probably have to just rub two sticks.

Tomb

T is for Tomb, an underground grave.
To go looking in here you've got to be brave.
There will be cobwebs, and spiders, and rats
and roaches, and beetles, and maybe some bats.

Why would you go in here if it's really not safe?
And since it's so wrong to walk into a grave?
Secrets are hidden in tombs such as these,
because no one would dare go in there, you see?

They're filled with bugs and ick and ewww.
And they probably smell quite terrible, too.
So, if you go in, you'll be holding your nose
and watching your step protecting your toes.

It's dark and it's scary so you'll want a light
to see everything that goes bump in the night.
It's probably nothing that's groaning all funny.
But you never quite know. It could be a mummy.

Underwater

U is for Underwater, the ocean or sea.
If you're looking for treasure that's where it will be.
It's sitting in chests or locked deep in a wreck
and there's no way to get it without getting wet.

There's gold and there's silver, in chunks and dabloons
and it's spread all over near reefs and lagoons.
There are antiques and trinkets, which are worth quite a bit.
And all of it, all of it, went down with the ship.

How did it get there? Down there so deep?
A storm, or some pirates, or the ship struck a reef.
Long ago treasure was carried by ships
that weren't very good at surviving their trips.

They'd tip and they'd sink—to the bottom they'd go,
holding a fortune in cargos of gold.
So put on your fins and take a deep breath.
There's treasure down there, just watch your step.

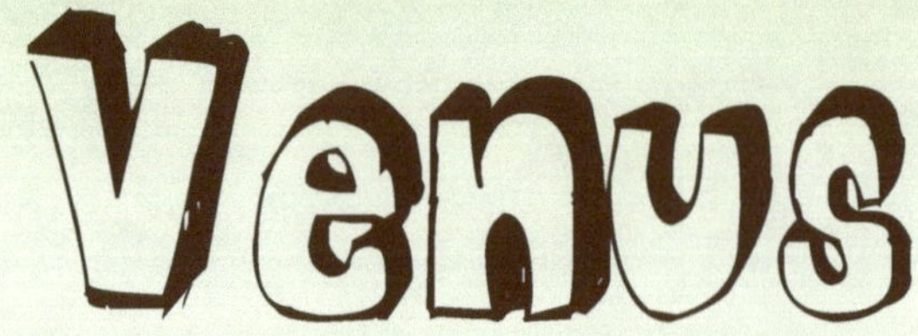

Venus

V is for Venus, a planet away.
No one's ever been there, but there will come a day
when we set foot on the soil of a place not our own
and adventure will follow in this great unknown.

A rocket will take us. There's no other way
to get to a place that's so far away.
And when we set down and take one step outside
there is no telling what we will find.

The land could be barren, boring and flat
or rolling and covered with weird kinds of plants.
And what of the people that live in this place?
Are there other people in outer space?

There could be aliens waiting to meet us.
There could be aliens waiting to eat us.
Will they have faces that smile when they see us?
Or is smiling just a weird thing to do when on Venus?

There will come days when we travel the stars.
And you've got to remember, when you travel that far,
to take everything that you'll need in your pack
because, when you're that far away, there's no going back.

W is for Wall, and the biggest there is
can be found in the East and has been there for years.
The Great Wall of China, that's what it's called,
is up to, in some places, thirty feet tall!

But that's not why it's grand. That's not why it's great.
The Great Wall of China runs all over the place.
For five thousand miles and five hundred more
the wall starts in the mountains and runs to the shore.

It's more than a wall, that much is true,
with guard houses and towers so they can watch you.
On top of the wall is a path that's so wide
that you and three friends can walk side by side.

And unlike the walls that hold up your roof
the great wall was made to hold back some troops.
It stood against armies and raiders and robbers
and for thousands of years no force could cross it.

If you go to China and feel like a walk,
you can follow the wall till you fall over and drop.
It goes on forever over rivers, around lakes.
It's just one of the things that makes it so great.

X marks the spot

X marks the Spot, you're finally here.
The thing that you've searched for is finally near.
It wasn't easy. There was lots in your way.
But you've finally reached it. Hip hip hooray.

You crossed rivers with hippos and fish that could bite.
You've done research and hiking and stayed up all night.
You've climbed mountains with sherpas and avoided the Yeti.
You've escaped from the cannibals without becoming spaghetti.

You've wandered the desert and been shipwrecked alone.
You've run from gorillas but instead of go home,
you pushed on through quicksand and survived a monsoon.
Now just reach that X. It will be over soon.

Because X is the spot that you've wanted to get.
All the clues and the hints say, "Yep. This is it."
So pick up your shovel and a pick for good measure.
Now start the digging and find that lost treasure.

Y is for Yak. So, there you have that.

Zeppelin

Z is for Zeppelin, a ship of the skies.
This is how you'll get home when you've collected your prize.
It floats like a balloon, but moves like a plane
and drifts along slowly 'till you're home again.

It may not be fast but it's mighty enough
to carry you safely and all of your stuff.
And you'll find it comfy to sleep in your berth
as the ship carries you home crossing the Earth.

You can dream about all of the things you have seen
or dream about all the places you've been.
You can dream about treasure, silver and gold
or dream of the excitement your next adventure will hold.

Benjamin Wallace is the father of three and thinks he can draw.

www.BenjaminWallaceBooks.com

www.ingramcontent.com/pod-product-compliance
Lightning Source LLC
Chambersburg PA
CBHW042116030726
47599CB00002B/233